W9-CSB-566

Thunder and Lightning

Helen Cox Cannons

Heinemann
LIBRARY
Chicago, Illinois

© 2015 Heinemann Library
an imprint of Capstone Global Library, LLC
Chicago, Illinois

Edited by Siân Smith and John-Paul Wilkins
Designed by Philippa Jenkins and Peggie Carley
Picture research by Ruth Blair
Production by Victoria Fitzgerald
Originated by Capstone Global Library Ltd
Printed and bound in China by Leo Paper Group

18 17 16 15 14
10 9 8 7 6 5 4 3 2 1

Library of Congress Cataloging in Publication Data
Cataloging-in-publication information is on file with the Library
of Congress.
ISBN 978-1-4846-0548-6 (hardcover)
ISBN 978-1-4846-0558-5 (paperback)
ISBN 978-1-4846-0573-8 (eBook PDF)

Photo Credits
Corbis: JGI/Jamie Grill/Blend Images, 19, Olix Wirtinger, 20;
Dreamstime: Bandesz, 18, 23 (bottom), Jhaz, 5; iStockphoto:
cschoeps, 15; NASA: 22 (left); Shutterstock: Andrey Prokhorov,
16, Balazs Kovacs, 12, 23 (middle), David W. Leindecker, 14,
Igor Zh., 22 (right), Mihai Simonia, 7, muratart, 13, Pictureguy,
4, Piotr Krzeslak, 21, Scott Prokop, 17, szpeti, 6, 23 (top),
violetkaipa, cover

We would like to thank John Horel for his invaluable help in the
preparation of this book.

Every effort has been made to contact copyright holders of
material reproduced in this book. Any omissions will be rectified
in subsequent printings if notice is given to the publisher.

Contents

What Is Thunder?

Thunder is the sound of **lightning**. You cannot see thunder, but you can hear it.

4

Thunder can sound like a low rumble or a loud crack.

What Is Lightning?

Lightning is a bright flash of **electricity** in the sky.

Lightning comes from a cloud.
A storm with thunder or lightning
is called a thunderstorm.

How Does Lightning Happen?

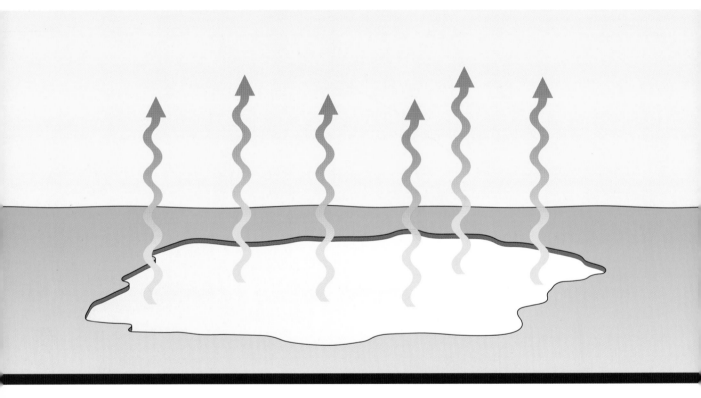

When the Sun warms water, some water becomes a gas called **vapor**. Vapor rises into the air.

The rising water vapor cools and forms a cloud. As more vapor rises, the cloud gets bigger and bigger.

Frozen raindrops inside the cloud start to bump into each other.

As they bump into each other, the frozen raindrops make electricity. This electricity turns into lightning.

When Does Lightning Happen?

Lightning can happen when it is warm.

Lightning can happen when it rains.

Types of Lightning

Sometimes lightning stays in a cloud.

Sometimes lightning strikes the ground.

Keeping Safe

Lightning can be very dangerous.

Lightning often strikes high places or tall things.

If you hear thunder, it means that lightning is close by.

It is best to stay inside when you
hear thunder.

What Is Good About Thunder and Lightning?

Thunder and lightning can be exciting.

Thunderstorms help us see the power of weather.

21

Did You Know?

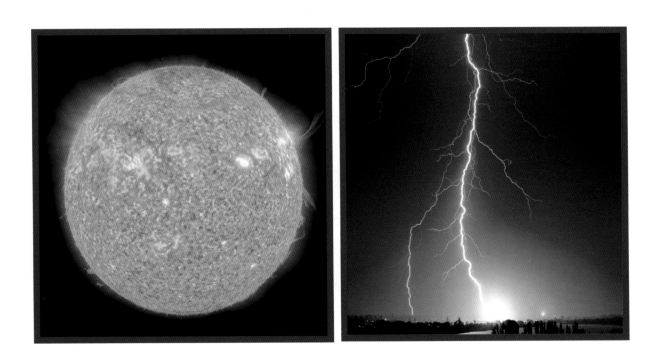

Lightning is about six times hotter than the Sun!

Picture Glossary

electricity form of energy

lightning bright flash of electricity in the sky

thunder the sound of lightning

vapor gas created by heating water

Index

Notes for Parents and Teachers

Before Reading

Assess background knowledge. Ask: What are thunder and lightning? Where do thunder and lightning come from?

After Reading

Recall and reflection: Ask children if their ideas about thunder and lightning at the beginning were correct. What else do they wonder about?

Sentence knowledge: Ask children to find sentences that end with three different punctuation marks. How does punctuation change the way they read sentences?

Word recognition: Have children point at the word *strikes* on page 15. Can they also find it on page 17?